# The
# 21st Century Classroom

# Creating Engaging eLessons
# for Every Student

By: Monica Sevilla

# CONTENTS:

# Chapter 1:

# The 21st Century Classroom

Most traditional schools have changed very little in terms of instruction and how students are educated.  Even though we live in a 21st century world marked by modern technology, traditional schools lag behind in terms of the instruction of technology that most modern businesses and companies commonly use today. Many of these school districts, for one reason or another,  are not equipped with laptop computers, tablets, mobile devices, software, applications and/or internet access to bring our students classrooms into the 21st century. Some school districts have the technology but have not changed their educational system and policies to allow for fluid integration of technology as a learning tool in the curriculum, and having students use this technology on a daily basis.

If  we, as educators, are to assist our students in becoming academically and skillfully competitive for entry level positions in the future job market, we need to teach them 21st century skills today. The most effective way to do this is through web-based learning.  Many careers today make use of computer technology and the Web to conduct business, to communicate with people around the world, and to run companies efficiently.  It is only practical that we our students learn these skills early and frequently to ensure that they are fully prepared for these opportunities.

Our students are still being taught with 20th century skills in the 20th century classroom. The educational paradigm must shift to allow students to learn 20th century skills across the curriculum at every grade level. The The one size fits all curriculum, based mainly on a physical textbook and the teacher as the "sage on the stage" is no longer an effective instructional model for our students today.  We need to transform our approach for the benefit of our students.

# What are 21st Century Learning skills?

21st century skills are at the heart of web-based learning.  They are defined as the essential skills needed for success in today's world. Students today must master specific skills, core content knowledge and expertise to succeed in work and life. Specific 21st century skills students will need to master include but are not limited to:

Communication skills (speaking and writing), conveying ideas to others

Literacy, reading , and comprehension skills, summarizing, note-taking

Critical thinking, problem solving, defining a problem and its variables, making decisions

Higher order thinking skills (analyzing, evaluating, synthesizing, ability to see connections and patterns, correlations, cause and effect, compare and contrast, similarities and differences, grouping, sorting, classifying, prioritizing, interpreting data and graphs) planning.

Innovativeness, creativity, inventiveness, originality, developing new ideas

Collaboration, cooperative learning, group learning, working as a team, resolving conflict, guiding others

Web-Based research, finding, using information from multiple sources, evaluating information

# Teaching 21st Century Skills

21st century skills can easily be incorporated into authentic projects that simulate real life situations and problems.   Projects are not only effective assessment tools to measure  core content knowledge, they are essentially powerful teaching opportunities enabling students to demonstrate their knowledge and application of the skills they have learned.   This is the opportunity many of our students need to practice and hone critical thinking and problem solving skills in a safe, nurturing environment, in preparation for life.  Projects fundamentally allow teachers to monitor and assess the proper use, application,  and mastery of skills.

 Authentic projects allow students the ability to demonstrate the higher order thinking skills attributed to Bloom's Taxonomy such as synthesizing, analyzing, and evaluating.   Employers today have seen a shortage of skilled students transitioning from our colleges and universities into the workforce.  Their most common concern is that students have not been taught adequate critical thinking and problem solving skills.  They state that our younger generation are not given enough novel and relevant experiences and real world situations to deal with.  They lack the experiential opportunities that ultimately build success and inner confidence.

We must not forget why we are educators. We prepare our students for life.  We teach them how to be life-long learners.  We show them how to think for themselves. and make informed decisions.  We are their models for how to conduct themselves as children and as adults.  We prepare them for their futures in the workplace and in society even though they may not know or understand how they fit into the bigger picture. The students need adults who have learned from their prior experiences and who can lead, motivate, and support them. They need us.

# Expectations for 21st Century Learners

If students are to learn 21st century skills, they must have high as well as clear expectations for their learning. High and clear expectations, with the proper scaffolding and support, motivates students to always improve and learn new knowledge and skills. It gives the students the clear message that they must master new knowledge and skills to be successful in both the short (now) and in the long term (future). The goal here is to create a cycle of continuous learning for every student.

Expectations need to be crystal clear and comprehensible. As a result, students will be able to clearly envision how their education (knowledge and skills) will directly benefit them in the workplace. The student will understand that the outcome of their education is having a rewarding career and a better quality of life. They will recognize that their education has prepared them for the career they desire.

A teacher who has low expectations for their students is a teacher who does not care about their progress and growth as an individual. To give students low expectations is the same as telling them they can not achieve their goals or master the knowledge and or skills they are learning. It creates a lack of motivation and an apathetic attitude towards the learning process. This degenerates into unwanted behavior on the part of the students, and stressful nightmare situations for teachers in the classroom.

Save yourself the grief and the headaches from the very beginning. Keep your expectations consistently clear and high throughout the school year.

# Chapter 2:

# Creating the 21st Century Classroom

The ideal 21st century classroom has several important components that together function as a synergistic unit. One component can not exist without the interaction of the other. The 21 st century classroom I am referring includes an educator at the helm who is a "facilitator of learning" who is savvy with computer hardware, software, and the use of the internet. A technology-ready classroom also contains at least one laptop or desktop computer for each learner, the appropriate computer applications to be used in the production of learning projects, and access to the internet. Macbook laptops are recommended for their versatility and convenience of their software for multimedia learning and their availability of technology such as built in cameras, etc. A technology coordinator is vital to the operating of computer hardware and software trouble-shooting. The last, and most crucial component, is the learner. Without the learner, education is not possible.

The 21st classroom should be set up with student collaboration in mind. Students need to be sitting together in pairs or in groups of four. Both configurations are acceptable in that they facilitate discussion and communication between "pairs" or partners. Students should be able to conveniently converse and share their ideas and thoughts with their partners. Research shows that ELL students who are given the opportunity to share discourse with each other improve dramatically in their communication skills and on standardized testing.

Student collaboration and communication are at the heart of the 21st Century curriculum. These are vital skills students will need to possess and refine for the future. Many employers will be looking for evidence of these skills in the workplace. Interestingly enough, collaboration and communication, especially writing, are two key entry level skills vital to the business world. Students who do not cultivate these skills will often not be hired or last in a position until they are promoted.

The educator, or teacher, will develop a curriculum that will allow students to work collaboratively in groups. Students will use their computers, resources posted on an educational website, developed by the educator, and other websites on the web as learning resources. They will complete learning tasks given to them by the within the time allotted to them in class. The educator will circulate among the student groups, monitor their progress, listen in on their academic conversation, offer input, and help with trouble shooting. As you can see, the role of the educator is one that is a "facilitator of learning," not the "sage on the stage. Here you are creating a community of learners.

Once the 21st century has been properly set up, the educator can now take into account the 21st century learning strategies that will work best with learning both core content knowledge and technology skills students will need to access in their future. The strategies the educator chooses must also support the delivery of an engaging and dynamic curriculum. 21st century learning strategies include: web-based learning, collaborative learning, and interactive learning.

# Chapter 3:
# Developing the 21st Century Curriculum

The 21st Century curriculum integrates the Common Core State Standards and 21st century skills together. They are reflected in every lesson and activity the students engage in and produce in the classroom. The vital components of the curriculum include the following:

Unit Lessons in Powerpoint or an eBook (PDF) format.
Assessments and Quizzes
eNotebooks such as interactive notebooks in Word or Lab Book
Blogs as written warm-ups
Projects
Assignments
Activities
Homework
Student ePortfolios
multimedia resources and interactive websites

Use of the Web for research

# The Standards-based Lesson

With the onset of NCLB in 2001 and the adoption of the Common Core State Standards, it is important that all teachers have knowledge of these standards, develop a solid standards-based curriculum, and successfully deliver this curriculum to all learners. Standards-based instruction focuses on the common Core and content area standards being taught and deciding what is essential for the student to learn. Here lies the challenge. What is important for your students to know in the first place? These are discussions that must take place with your colleagues to develop the common understandings of what is essential and what is not. Some of the questions you should ask are:

1) What should the students know and be able to do (skills) according to the standard.

2) What essential ideas or big ideas should they know this year and for sub sequent years (vertical articulation)

3) What do they need to know for life?

Once you have identified what the students should know and be able to do, and what is essential for your students to know, then you can develop a curriculum composed of standards-based lessons. You can use the **Standards-Based Lesson Plan Template** created just for this purpose.

# Developing a Standards-based Lesson

Standards-based instruction focuses on the standards and what is essential for the student to learn. Before developing your lessons, decide what the goal and objective for each of the standards being taught. Then, develop a task or product that will demonstrate their mastery of the standard(s) being used.

**Goal:** The Main Standard

**Objective:** What about the Main Standard do you want your students to learn? What should they know or be able to do? (the substandard)

**Task:** What activity will you have the students do in class to achieve the objective? (on this day)

Goal ----------->Objective------------>Task (Product)

# Standards-based Lesson Planning Guide

*Goal (s): What standard(s) do students need to know.*

*Objective (s): What do students need to know or be able to do?(steps to mastery of the standard)*

*Task (s): What task(s )/products will the student create that demonstrates the student has accomplished the objective.*
*note: task(s) done in one one day of teaching*

*Technology: What technology will you use and how will you use it to drive your lesson?*

*Teaching and SDAIE Strategies Used. What research based strategies/SDAIE strategies will I use to teach this lesson.*

*Concept Vocabulary for this lesson:*

*Assessment (s): Which assessments will you use to assess prior knowledge and measure whether the student has mastered the standard.*

*Reflection: How would I improve the implementation of this lesson?*

*Re-teaching and Intervention: What will I do when all students have not learned?*

# Helpful Tips for Developing A Lesson

✦ 1) Decide what essential ideas students should know and what essential skills they will need to perform based on the standard (s).

✦2) Decide what type of product (i.e. a an article or an eBook about a unit of study), the students will create to demonstrate mastery of the standard (s).

✦3) Decide which levels of Bloom's taxonomy are appropriate based on the standard.

✦ 4 Consider the ELD levels of my students? What language development activities will I use so my students can access the core content.

✦ 5) Decide what computer programs and applications will be appropriate for both you and the student to use during the lesson. (I.e Word, Powerpoint, ) plan guide on the next page.

✦ 6) Decide how you will assess your students for mastery of the standards (I.e. through an exam, creation of a project)

✦7) Decide what key vocabulary the students need to learn and have them spend time learning the terms (eDictionaries and eFlashcards in Powerpoint or in ComicLife)

✦8) Decide what resources or supplemental help you will offer students if they have not mastered the standards.

✦9) Offer enrichment opportunities and activities for students who have mastered the standards and want to learn more about a topic (i.e. virtual field trips, WebQuests)

✦10) To help you plan your lesson with these tips in mind, use the standards-based lesson

# Creating Projects

Creating projects is the most effective assessment of learning concepts and skills. Research shows that students who are able to demonstrate their learning in projects developed at the "Creating" level of Bloom's Taxonomy are able to retain the information longer and score higher on the standardized tests. In leu of having students show that they mastered knowledge and skills on a paper-based exam or cumulative final, research or inquiry projects can be used instead. These projects are a more authentic way of assessing the skills of remembering, understanding, applying, analyzing, and evaluating key concepts and skills for a unit or period of study.

21st century skills can easily be incorporated into authentic web-based projects that simulate real life situations and problems. Projects are not only effective assessment tools to measure core content knowledge, they are essentially powerful teaching opportunities enabling students to demonstrate their knowledge and application of the skills they have learned. Projects fundamentally allow teachers to monitor and assess the proper use, application, and mastery of skills.

Authentic projects also allow students the ability to learn the higher order thinking skills attributed to Bloom's Taxonomy such as synthesizing, analyzing, and evaluating. This is the learning opportunity many of our students need to practice and hone critical thinking and problem solving skills in a safe, nurturing environment, in preparation for life. Employers today have seen a shortage of skilled students transitioning from our colleges and universities into the workforce. Their most common concern is that students have not been taught adequate critical thinking and problem solving skills. They state that our younger generation are not given enough novel and relevant experiences and real world situations to deal with. They lack the experiential opportunities that ultimately build success and inner confidence.

The beauty of this type of assignment is that they incorporate the problem solving and critical thinking skills found in the "applying", "analyzing", and "evaluating" levels of Bloom's Taxonomy along with understanding and comprehending the basic knowledge and skills in the "remembering" and "understanding" levels.  Projects created at this level are well rounded, well planned, incorporate a dynamic range of tasks and assignments that students can see how they inter-connect together to form the "big picture" in the minds of our students.  Excellent examples of projects that can be given to students at the "creating" level include:  Publishing (eBooks, interactive eNotebooks, eMagazines,  ePortfolios, eJournals, articles, iMovies, video casting, podcasting, creating multimedia presentations such as Powerpoint and Keynote, and broadcasting.

# Creating Student eProjects

Creating eProjects is the most effective assessment of learning concepts and skills. Research shows that students who are able to demonstrate their learning in projects developed at the "Creating" level of Bloom's Taxonomy are able to retain the information longer and score higher on the standardized tests. In leu of having students show that they mastered knowledge and skills on a paper-based exam or cumulative final, research or inquiry projects can be used instead. These projects are a more authentic way of assessing the skills of remembering, understanding, applying, analyzing, and evaluating key concepts and skills for a unit or period of study.

21st century skills can easily be incorporated into authentic web-based projects that simulate real life situations and problems. Projects are not only effective assessment tools to measure core content knowledge, they are essentially powerful teaching opportunities enabling students to demonstrate their knowledge and application of the skills they have learned. Projects fundamentally allow teachers to monitor and assess the proper use, application, and mastery of skills.

Authentic projects also allow students the ability to learn the higher order thinking skills attributed to Bloom's Taxonomy such as synthesizing, analyzing, and evaluating. This is the learning opportunity many of our students need to practice and hone critical thinking and problem solving skills in a safe, nurturing environment, in preparation for life. Employers today have seen a shortage of skilled students transitioning from our colleges and universities into the workforce. Their most common concern is that students have not been taught adequate critical thinking and problem solving skills. They state that our younger generation are not given enough novel and relevant experiences and real world situations to deal with. They lack the experiential opportunities that ultimately build success and inner confidence.

The beauty of this type of assignment is that they incorporate the problem solving and critical thinking skills found in the "applying", "analyzing", and "evaluating" levels of Bloom's Taxonomy along with understanding and comprehending the basic knowledge and skills in the "remembering" and "understanding" levels.  Projects created at this level are well rounded, well planned, incorporate a dynamic range of tasks and assignments that students can see how they inter-connect together to form the "big picture" in the minds of our students.  Excellent examples of projects that can be given to students at the "creating" level include:  Publishing (eBooks, interactive eNotebooks, eMagazines,  ePortfolios, eJournals, articles, iMovies, video-casting, podcasting, and creating multimedia presentations.

# Creating Student ePortfolios

## What is a Student ePortfolio.

A student ePortfolio is an electronic portfolio that is created and maintained on a computer or posted on a website. The ePortfolio is folder with a collection of student work organized and kept within smaller categories of folders.

## Why Create Student ePortfolios?

Student ePortfolios are a great way to organize and store student work electronically on a computer.    The ePortfolio takes the place of the student's traditional notebook or folder and contains the student's lessons, assignments, assessments, projects, and more! The portfolio eliminates paper waste, and can be saved by the students on a CD or thumb drive. The portfolio can later be used for reviewing information learned later in the school year in preparation for State exams.

## How to Create an ePortfolio

There are a few different ways to create ePortfolios. The easiest way is to:

1. Create a folder by double clicking "new folder" from the "Finder" menu on a Mac computer.

2. The student's name can be added to the folder by clicking and holding the name "untitled folder" right under the folder icon and pressing the delete button. Add the student's name to the box.

3. To create folders for each category of student work you would like the ePortfolio to contain, create a new folder with the new category name, click & hold, and drag the folder into your main portfolio folder. Repeat the process for each category.

## Categories of Folders May include:

Unit Lessons in a Powerpoint presentation or an eBook (PDF) format.
Lecture Notes Assessments and Quizzes
Journals (writing assignments)
Class warm-ups
Worksheets
Pictures, photos, diagrams
Reports
Projects
Assignments/Activities
Homework
Lab Book

4. The folder can stay on the computer desktop or it can be burned onto a CD, saved onto a thumb drive, or uploaded onto a website.

For more ideas, visit the eClassroom 4 Teachers website at: https://sites.google.com/site/eclassroom4teachers/Home.

# Chapter 4

# Differentiating

# the 21st Century Curriculum

Differentiating the Curriculum is an educational approach that provides students with different ways to learn information. Students are individuals, have different learning needs, and construct meaning in different ways. Educators can offer their students a choice from a variety of different activities and projects developed with their needs in mind. The curriculum can be differentiated to reflect the following factors in mind:

-the type of learner (ELL, Special Needs, Gifted, Standard, At-Risk)
-the ability level (ie... math level, literacy level)
-student groupings (individuals, pairs, small groups)
-interests
-learning style
-learning product
-rigor or higher order thinking skills

One of the most important factors influencing the success of students on the Common Core State Standards exams is their proficiency in being able to apply content knowledge and comprehension to higher order thinking skills. The educator is forced to incorporate these skills as they develop their curriculum plan and lessons.

# Bloom's Taxonomy

*I*n 1956, Benjamin Bloom and a team of educational psychologists developed a classification or taxonomy of levels of cognitive skills for the development of thinking and learning. In the 1990's, a new group lead by Lorin Anderson (a former student of Bloom's. The group updated the taxonomy in reflection of work done 21st century . This is a new representation of Bloom's Taxonomy. Nouns have been changed to action words (Verbs) to describe the different levels. Action words more accurately depict the "active" nature of the process of learning.Oliver Wendell Holmes and Art Costa described it as:

"Before we can **understand** a concept we have to **remember** it
Before we can **apply** the concept we must **understand** it
Before we **analyze** it we must be able to **apply** it
Before we can **evaluate** its impact we must have **analyzed** it
Before we can **create** we must have **remembered, understood, applied, analyzed,** and **evaluated**."

This description outlines the process or pattern of thinking students follow to construct a meaningful framework for learning knowledge and skills. Certain learning objectives and tasks must be accomplished before others. Learning can start at any level in this process. Each level becomes "cumulative" of the knowledge and skills in the levels preceding it. Basic knowledge and skills are acquired at the "knowledge" and "understanding" levels of Bloom's taxonomy. This is where the foundation of learning is created.

How Do We Learn? We learn by constructing knowledge through following distinct "levels" of thinking described in Bloom's Taxonomy. The following is the new representation of Bloom's taxonomy:

**Remembering**
**Understanding**
**Applying**
**Analyzing**
**Evaluating**
**Creating**

# Bloom's Taxonomy in Detail

## Remembering:

Remembering knowledge and skills at the basic level of Bloom's taxonomy can be done by daily practice and its incorporation into the understanding of knowledge and skills in the next level and built into the routine. Activities can be in the form of memory aids, concept maps, and graphic organizers.These activities could be done the first 5-10 minutes in class as a warm-up or the last 5-10 minutes of class as a review or recap of what was learned that day. Remembering knowledge is the responsibility of the student to also practice at home.
examples:
define, duplicate, list, memorize, recall, repeat, reproduce, state

## Understanding:

Students must understand key concepts and skills before they are expected to apply and use it in novel situations. This is the expectation that society places on learners throughout their lives in the workplace. Students must be able to understand what they've learned and clearly communicate it to others.

Activities geared to the understanding and comprehension of key concepts in a unit of study should be carefully planned out and should directly support the main topic. Students should also be asked to demonstrate their understanding through a written assignment such as summarizing, describing, and identifying and in-class discussion, reporting out, and explaining so they gain the practice and experience in written communication and verbal expression.

Examples: classify, describe, discuss, explain, identify, locate, recognize, report, select, translate, paraphrase.

**Applying**:

Students, when they enter the workplace, must be able to take the knowledge they have learned and apply it in new ways. At this level, practice and opportunities to gain this practice becomes critical. An ample amount of time must be invested at this stage to ensure that the student develops these skills properly. The consequence of not doing so becomes devastating. Here is where the students first learn critical thinking and problem solving skills. The burden is placed squarely on the teacher to introduce strategies, tasks, and activities to develop and strengthen these skills. Best practices include giving students reflection questions they can answer and record in a notebook.

Questions can be related to cause and effect, extrapolate thinking, make predictions based on what you know, explain possible outcomes, and demonstrate your thinking. Questions should stimulate thinking and provoke thought.

Examples: choose, demonstrate, dramatize, employ, illustrate, interpret, operate, schedule, sketch, solve, use, **write**.

It is interesting to note that writing is listed as an example of a skill at the "applying" level. Let's examine why this is. Writing at this level not only incorporate the physical action of writing but also the metacognitive skill of writing. We are essential asking our students to recall what they have learned, explain what they know, apply this knowledge to new, novel situations or in a new format in written form. They are essentially using the information they have learned and communicating their thoughts and ideas to others. This is one of the main expectations society has deemed as an essential skill for hiring and promotion in the workforce. Students who are weak in this area encounter one of the harsh realities of life. The diminished availability of career options and opportunities.

If we are to sufficiently prepare our students for the future, we must first teach this skill with fidelity, and offer many opportunities to our students for the practice and development of this skill. Neglect and avoidance on our part will directly impact the future of our students. The consequences of our actions will result in our students inability to be hired or promoted by existing businesses for lack of the entry level skills needed to become successful employees. Their failure is our failure!

## Analyzing:

Students analyze or examine data, observations, and information they have, sort it into distinct categories to differentiate between them, and also recognize patterns that emerge. Students at this level are able to "see" the similarities and differences, and differentiate between types of data and observations. Students can then make informed decisions, judgments, and conclusions from it.
Examples: appraise, compare, contrast, criticize, differentiate, discriminate, distinguish, examine, experiment, **question**, test.

## Evaluating:

Students take the information and evidence they have analyzed, and make informed decisions, judgments, and conclusions from it. The student is able to defend, support, or make a judgment about a claim or position based on the data they have seen.
examples: appraise, **argue**, **defend**, judge, select, **support**, value, evaluate.

## Creating:

The level of "Creating" within the learning process incorporates all the levels proceeding it. The most effective learning projects for students are ones which they create, design, plan, and write themselves to demonstrate their mastery of key concepts and skills .

The fundamental critical thinking and problem solving skills students need to master are found in the "applying", "analyzing", and "evaluating" levels of Bloom's taxonomy. Once mastered, these skills ultimately work together in synergy and also complement one another in the "**Creating**" level of Bloom's taxonomy. It is at this level that students get the "most bang for their buck."

Most of the academic gains in standardized testing are the outcome of projects created by students at this level. These projects incorporate the the problem solving and critical thinking skills found in the "applying", "analyzing", and "evaluating" levels of Bloom's Taxonomy along with understanding and comprehending the basic knowledge and skills in the "remembering" and "understanding" levels. Projects created at this level are well rounded, well planned, incorporate a dynamic range of tasks and assignments that students can see how they inter-connect and all play an important role in the "big picture".

Thinking skills associated with the "Creating" level of Bloom's taxonomy: assemble, construct, create, design, develop, formulate, write, plan, produce, invent, devise, make.
Projects incorporating the following skills demonstrate learning at the highest level of Bloom's taxonomy, the "Creating" level:
Publishing (eBooks, eNotebooks, eMagazines, reports, ePortfolios, eJournals, articles, wikis, blogs, tweets, plans), animating, filming (making

movies), video casting, podcasting, creating multimedia presentations, and broadcasting.

# Differentiating Learning
# with Multiple Intelligences

Howard Gardner, an American psychologist, developed a theory he called "Multiple Intelligences" His theory clearly explains that people obtain different intelligences and can learn in a variety of different ways. Gardner suggests that schools should provide an education that is centered on the individual and the curriculum should be tailored to a student's intelligence profile. (Allan & Tomlinson, 2000). This is a kind of differentiated instruction is based on the different learning profiles of students.

Gardner asserts that students prefer to learn in 9 unique and different learning styles or intelligences. These styles of learning represent the mode of learning in which the students make strong neural connections with, and therefore, are most comfortable with. If we as educators realize this prospect, then it will also serve as a great predictor in which content areas our students academic strengths will lie in the future. These subject areas, most often than not, are usually the predictors of possible future career paths. The 9 intelligences include:

Verbal/Linguistic
Logical/Mathematical
Visual/Spatial
Musical/Rhythmic
Bodily/Kinesthetic
Naturalist
Interpersonal
Intrapersonal
Existential

Using the web is a great way to differentiate student learning. One way to individually "tailor" learning is to consider your students' multiple intelligences.

The most effective way to do this is to create or find resources that match with your student's dominant multiple intelligences. You can gather information and data by surveying your students and asking them what their preferred style of learning is and observing what sensory information motivates your students. You will then be able to design, create and choose the appropriate curricular resources to engage each of your students in learning. With technology such as computers, cameras, software, and web, content area concepts and skills can be presented in ways that appeal to the dominant intelligences of the students. In this way, a variety of presentations can be posted on a website for access by students.

We, as educators, take on the responsibility of cultivating and nurturing the development of these intelligences within our own classrooms. It is our responsibility to be aware of their dominant intelligences and find resources that will engage, motivate, and effectively help the student master key concepts and skills. It is also equally important to expose students to a variety of resources created for students with other intelligences as well. The reasoning for this is to develop and strengthen their non-dominant intelligences, make connections with other parts of the brain, and give them other learning experiences they can draw upon in the future.

# Differentiation Inventory

It is helpful for the differentiation of lessons to be carefully planned out to cover as many types of learners as possible. An inventory makes it easier to see the different possibilities for effective learning products.

Here is an example:

**8th Grade Physical Science Standard:** Students with apply simple mathematic relationships to determine a missing quantity in a mathematic expression, given the two remaining terms (including speed = distance/time, density = mass/volume, force = pressure × area, volume = area × height).

**Objective of the Lesson:** Students will successfully solve problems, step by step, applying the math formula:

$$Density = mass/volume$$

|  |  |
| --- | --- |
| type of learners | ELL |
| ability levels | English: far below basic<br>Math: far below basic |
| learning style | visual, auditory |
| level of rigor | application |
| student groupings | pairs |

| | |
|---|---|
| interests | animation, music, video games, multimedia |
| learning product | ? |

Now that the inventory is complete, the information can be analyzed and used to develop the appropriate learning product for your students. According to the learning objective, English language learners with far below basic ELA and Math skills will demonstrate their knowledge and understanding of the formula density = mass/volume and be able to apply this knowledge to solve problems in a step by step fashion.

To ensure students are able to "apply" this concept, they can perform a higher order thinking skill associated with the "Application" level of Bloom's taxonomy. Appropriate learning skills within this level include solving, showing, modeling, and applying density problems. Based on this information, students can:

"show other students how to solve density problems for unknown quantities to others"

Taking a quick look at their interests will tell us what types of activities or projects will engage students and can be used as a learning product. In this example, the inventory lists animation, music, videos, movies, games, and multimedia as interests for this age group. Possible activities and projects for students to complete include:

-making an animated movie
-making a movie with an iPhone or iPod
-recording a song
-creating a step by step "How To" multimedia Powerpoint or Keynote

presentation
-creating an interactive "How To" poster

Educators can also group their students in pairs or small groups.  ELL students need opportunities to develop their speaking and listening skills.  ELL students benefit and thrive when they are allowed converse and discuss with others.  To facilitate this communication, students can be paired or placed into small groups.  They can collaborate and figure out the best strategy to explain how to solve a step by step density problem.  Together, they can choose an activity or project that piques their interests as a group.  Educators may also enhance their ELA skills by requiring each group to complete a written component to their project and to present there project to the other members of the class.

# Differentiation Inventory Template

Standard:

Objective of the Lesson:

|  |  |
| --- | --- |
| type of learners | |
| ability levels | |
| learning style | |
| level of rigor | |
| student groupings | |
| interests | |
| learning product | |

# Using Technology to Differentiate the Curriculum

We are fortunate that we live in a time where we can use technology as both a curriculum development and instructional delivery tool. Educators can utilize the power of the Web to differentiate projects and activities for their students. Having a good foundation and working knowledge of computer and web applications and how they can be utilized in the learning process is essential to the successful implementation of activities and projects in the curriculum. Below is a table showing the more popular educational computer/web applications, examples of activities and projects students can create, and their purpose in education.

Technology can be altered to facilitate the differentiation of the curriculum. By altering certain key components, learning opportunities both inside and outside of the classroom can be created for all students. A website or blog that contains a combination of these technology tools allows students to extend access to the core curriculum and increases the learning time students can spend with their learning materials. Students can also interact with them quickly and conveniently by using their own personal mobile devices such as smartphones.

Websites also expose students to a variety of different resources they would not normally experience if they were solely to rely on just a textbook for learning. Their curriculum can be supplemented and enhanced to include more higher order thinking activities and projects requiring students to create products of learning on computer, web, and mobile applications. These student created projects demonstrating their mastery of concepts and skills can be used as assessments to measure and gauge how far the students have progressed in the learning process. Tools such as these prepare students for standardized exams by increasing the frequency and time students spend developing and practicing the skills they will be assessed on these tests.

Important technological elements include:

-websites
-blogs
-gadgets and widgets
-applications (computer, web-based, or mobile)
-use of mobile devices
- files such as documents, photos, images, audio, videos, movies, and multimedia
-RSS/Atom feeds

# Chapter 5:

# The eLesson

Teachers are always looking for new and novel ways to deliver the same instruction but in a more exciting and engaging way. Shifting from the traditional lecture format to using technology such as computers and mobile devices puts students in the driver's seat and puts them in charge of their own learning. By using technology, teachers can leverage learning innovative ways. Let's face it, the clientele has changed tremendously. Many of them are using their I Phones, I Pods, I Pads, and any other mobile device to call their friends, listen to music, text message, surf the net, play games. take photos, and the list goes on and on! Why not use these devices to your advantage? Students are already familiar with how these devices operate. Why not take it one step further and allow students to learn about your subject material by accessing it with their mobile devices?

Be Creative! You can create a lesson in eBook format, called an eLesson. eLessons can be posted on your teacher website in PDF format, and students can access it via the internet from school or at home. Students can access your website, download your eLesson, and learn at their own pace with their mobile devices. You will have literally put learning in their own hands!

One of the simplest ways to create an eLesson is as a Multimedia presentation in Powerpoint or Keynote to do. Educators can easily add text, images, and audio to their presentations, convert them into Quicktime movies and post them on their class websites and/or You Tube. Other educators, myself included, enjoy creating PDFs (eBooks), posting them on a class website, and publishing them via Amazon.com and Barnes & Noble for others to use and enjoy.

# Simple Instructions for Creating eLessons in Powerpoint

Projects can be created in Powerpoint by following this simple format:

1. Open the Powerpoint application by clicking on the icon. Click the "Powerpoint Presentation" box in the project gallery. The application will launch a blank template which can be considered your "canvas".

2. Save your presentation under the "File"menu.

3. To add pages in the presentation, you will add slides to the Powerpoint project.
Dedicate the first slide as the Title page to the presentation. On this page add:

*the title of the presentation *a picture, photo, or animation *Name of the author (s) of the presentation
Start creating the project by adding slides/pages to it. On each page/slide add:

*1-2 sentences of the presentation.
*A picture, photo, animation or a video
*Audio recording with narration of the story
*Music (MP3 format) (optional)

4. Add action buttons to each page to link them and be able to "flip" through the presentation by clicking the buttons.

# eLessons in All Shapes and Sizes

eLessons can be created for different purposes. You may want your students to learn the meat and potatoes of a unit of study. In this case, it would make sense if your eLesson contains the core content material at hand, assignments, pre- and post- assessments, and other projects for your students to complete. You may also want to focus on learning the vocabulary terms of the unit of study. An eDictionary eBook, or a book containing the vocabulary terms, their definitions, and pictures would be appropriate for this purpose. You may also want to create an eBook about a specific topic within the unit of study but go into depth and have your students read it as an enrichment assignment. All of these are possibilities. Having your students create their own eBook project, one form of eProject, is another possibility.

A one size fits all learning system is no longer an appropriate instructional model. Every student can not learn the same content, in the exact same way, and at the exact same time. Each of our students are unique. Even though they may be in the same age group, their individual academic needs are vastly different from each other. Students vary in their ethnic and cultural backgrounds, their interests, their experiences, their academic preparedness, and their use of technology. For these reasons, differentiating the learning experience is important for our students.

A curriculum that has been differentiated to become student centered, rigorous, tailored to specific learning styles and interests of the students maximize and accelerate their learning. Research shows that students who create learning projects and spend more of their instructional time in the classroom applying higher order thinking skills retain information longer and perform better on standardized tests. It is important to allow students to choose a learning experience that is engaging and appropriate for them. It enables them to select a product of learning, or a project that demonstrates their mastery of the concepts and skills, that motivates them. Allowing students this freedom of choice increases the chances that they will complete and submit a product successfully for credit.

Maximizing the learning experiences of an array of different learners to the fullest extent possible requires educators to adopt and utilize a significantly different approach to teaching. This may require educators to abandon practices that are not successful and replace them with more different practices in order to adapt the learning environment to effectively meet the needs of our students. This also may require educators to move from the more traditional classroom setting to a classroom atmosphere that is set up to facilitate groups of students sharing, collaborating, problem solving, and learning together with the use of technology as a tool.

Here are a few ideas of different eLessons that can be created with Microsoft Office and iWork tools:

1. Multimedia Presentation Software such as Powerpoint and Keynote. Presentations and slideshows can then be converted into Quicktime Movies or eBooks (PDF).

2. Word and Pages can be used to generate eBooks, reports, magazines, newsletters, cards, posters, flyers, Ads, brochures, menus, calendars in .doc, PDF, or ePub formats.

3. Excel and Numbers can be used to make charts, diagrams, tables, forms, organizers, grades books, databases, inventory, lists, and calculation tools in .xls or PDF formats.

# Chapter 6

# eBooks

The eBook is a wonderful way to publish your written works quickly and conveniently. They can be available to the public with the click of a button. The eBook is merely a written book available in electronic or digital format. Many publishers now offer books in print as well as in electronic or digital form. The eBook is created and written in a word processing application, converted to a PDF or an ePub file, uploaded onto an online publisher's website, and sold to prospective readers. Many books in print have been digitalized and posted online as eBooks.

Many professions now exist online through the use of the Internet that didn't 20 years ago. One such profession is ePublishing or writing and publishing books in electronic or digital format. writing articles for websites, blogs, and eBooks. With the convenience of internet access and online publishers, anyone could write and publish in their pajamas and submit their written works to their employers and publishers from home.

The good news here is that students (as well as adults) could learn relevant ePublishing skills, namely writing, communication tools, and web skills within minutes, and be able to use them fluidly. It is not limited to age. For students, the skills and guidelines they would need for ePublishing profession in the future, can be easily be taught through assignments, activities, and projects they do in their content areas. These assignments and activities can be developed to simulate what they would encounter in the workplace such as a career in ePublishing. Preparing our students with

21st century skills is of the upmost importance. The more real life experiences and opportunities they are given in the classroom now, the more successful they will be in the real world in the future. Students will be able to directly translate their ePublishing skills to jobs requiring specific skills in computer technology and writing. Ask yourself this vital question: How many jobs in the future will require the knowledge and training computer technology skills?

There are many practical uses for eBooks in the field of Education. eBooks are powerful tools that teachers can create for the instruction of core content knowledge to be accessed by the student. eBooks created by the students help them demonstrate their mastery of content skills and also strengthen their verbal and written communication skills. The practical uses of eBooks are many. One important use of eBooks is its ability to engage students in the skill and the art of writing. The more writing opportunities teachers make available to their students, the more practice they will get, and the more confident they will become.

Teachers can create eBook unit lessons or eLessons as PDFs and post them on their websites for students to download. eBook lessons may contain the unit lesson, images, vocabulary terms to know, assignments, and assessments. eBook documents created in Word, Pages, Powerpoint and Keynote all suffice and can be converted to PDF files. The practical uses of eLessons is that students can access the content within the lesson and learn at their own pace. They are also able to access this information 24/7, from home, and during the summer. Learning can take place anytime, anywhere.

eBooks serve as a product of student learning and mastery of subject area content that can be monitored and assessed. eBooks allow students to demonstrate content knowledge and skills learned over a specified period of time. eBooks can be used in leu of the traditional paper-based project. Book reports, science fair reports, content area reports, and cross-curricular reports requiring web-based research can naturally be created and saved as an eBook.  It's a great way to "go green", save a few trees, and create a product that can be saved in digital format.

The most powerful educational research-based instructional strategy is allowing students to become the masters or the authors of their own learning.   Research shows that teachers who implement  a curriculum (namely activities, and projects) that requires students to use the higher order levels of Bloom's taxonomy, help them to learn, remember, and master the content of a subject area more efficiently.  Students also improve their communication skills (verbal and written) dramatically.Higher order thinking skills, such as creating eBooks  and other ePublishing projects, also allow students to develop and practice critical thinking skills. Projects like these engage and motivate the students, effectively lowering opportunities for misbehavior. curricular reports requiring web-based research can naturally be created and saved as an eBook.  It's a great way to "go green", save a few trees, and create a product that can be saved in digital format.

# Tips for Creating Simple eBooks

1. Choose the topic the students will focus in their eBook. Be certain to add the ELA goals for reading, writing, and communication for their grade level.

2. Decide what criteria the students will meet and what they will write about in their eBook project to demonstrate their mastery of the content knowledge and skills for the topic they are presently learning.     This can be done by having students write about and research the major learning objectives for the topic they are learning.

3. Develop a rubric for grading your students  eBook project.

4. Choose a computer software that is easy to manage and that offers many writing, editing,  and graphic tools such as Word, Pages, Powerpoint or Keynote.   The writing process does not need to be complicated by using software that will cause a lot of grief and headaches in the long run.

5. Write a brief set of instructions, based on the criteria you have developed for the eBook for your students.

6. Walk them through the major features of  the application your students will be using.
    Go through the eProject  instructions you have written with your students step by step.

7. Have your students create the cover, title page, and content page for

their eBook.  Next have them save their work.

8.      Have your students write the major sections (chapters) including text pages and picture pages for their book according to the criteria you set in their instructions.

9.      Have your students select pictures from searching in Google images and have them drag & drop them into their book  project.

9.      When they are finished with their eBook, have them save  their work as a PDF.


These documents can be easily be converted to a PDF  and saved by going to the "File" menu of the application you are working with, clicking on print, and choosing the "Save as PDF button". Have your students save your PDF  when they are finished with their project on your desktop, in separate folder, or on a thumb drive. Many documents can be saved in this standardized format, posted on websites  or sent to others without the fuss!

# Chapter 7

# Digital Storybooks

## Writing Stories

A story is term used for describing, in verbal or written form, a sequence of events or facts. It is defined as a tale or narrative of real (fiction) or non-real (non-fiction) events. A story can be about an event, person, or an experience. A story usually contains characters who interact, over a specific period of time, and in a specific geographic place.

Both fiction and non-fiction stories can be written. Students can create and write storybooks across the curriculum in the core content areas as a project demonstrating their mastery of key concepts and skills. Teachers can decide which story style, fiction or non-fiction, would be appropriate to use in a project. This would depend on the core content area and the key concept or skill being taught.

## Creating Digital Storybooks Using Powerpoint

Powerpoint is the most heavily used presentation applications in education. Used for its versatility and practical uses, this learning tool is a favorite among educators and students alike. Text, images, animations, videos and recordings of voice and music can all be integrated into a dynamic presentation to be shown to others. It transforms textual information into an engaging multimedia experience.

Powerpoint has many practical uses in the curriculum. The saavy teacher can create their content lessons and assignments on Powerpoint, present it to their students during class as part of their instruction, and also post it on their websites online. Students are able to create projects to demonstrate their learning such as reports, documentaries, journals, science fair projects, photo albums, student portfolios, eDictionaries, flashcards, games and concept reviews.

Teachers and students can easily create digital storybooks on Powerpoint (or Macintosh Keynote). Its versatility and practical uses, this learning tool is a favorite among educators and students alike. Text, images, animations, videos and audio recordings can all be integrated into a dynamic multimedia presentation, transforming textual information into an visually engaging experience. Powerpoint can be navigated with a person reading the story at their own pace, or can be set to slide presentation mode where the slides automatically change after a designated amount of time.

# Instructions for Creating
# Digital Storybooks in Powerpoint

Storybooks can be created in Powerpoint by following this simple format:

1. To Create pages in the storybook, you will add slides to the Powerpoint presentation.

2. Dedicate the first slide as the cover to the story book. On this page add:
   *the title of the book
   *a picture, photo, or animation
   *Name of the author (s) of the storybook

3. Start writing the story by adding slides/pages to the storybook. On each page/slide add:
   *1-2 sentences of the story.
   *A picture, photo, animation or a video
   *Audio recording with narration of the story
   *Music (MP3 format) (optional)

4. Add buttons to each page to link them and be able to "flip" through the book by clicking the buttons.

# Digital Storybook Projects

Creating projects is the most effective assessment of learning concepts and skills. Research shows that students who are able to demonstrate their learning in projects developed at the "Creating" level of Bloom's Taxonomy are able to retain the information longer and score higher on the standardized tests. In leu of having students show that they mastered knowledge and skills on a paper-based exam or cumulative final, research or inquiry projects can be used instead. These projects are a more authentic way of assessing the skills of remembering, understanding, applying, analyzing, and evaluating key concepts and skills for a unit or period of study. Students can create these types of projects individually, or in collaboration with their peers.

The beauty of this type of assignment is that they incorporate the problem solving and critical thinking skills found in the "applying", "analyzing", and "evaluating" levels of Bloom's Taxonomy along with understanding and comprehending the basic knowledge and skills in the "remembering" and "understanding" levels. Projects created at this level are well rounded, well planned, incorporate a dynamic range of tasks and assignments that students can see how they inter-connect together to form the "big picture" in the minds of our students.

Writing assignments should also be designed at the higher levels of Bloom's taxonomy such as "creating", "evaluating, and "analyzing." This will ensure they are writing at a high enough level to practice and develop critical thinking and problem-solving skills on a daily basis. As easily as digital stories can be downloaded and read from a website containing children's storybooks, students can create their own digital storybooks with the use of a computer or I Pad, and Powerpoint or Keynote as a student project.

# Chapter 8

# Creating Movies, Videos & Podcasts

Movies are a global iconic multimedia that has been used as a communication tool for disseminating information and for entertainment purposes, but also as an important learning tool. Movies that are created by students  them to use their imaginations to invent a story, plan their stories, organize their ideas, and write a script of dialogue or narration for the story.  These skills, standing alone, are higher level thinking skills used in the movie making process. Students will also thread higher order thinking skills to construct knowledge the concepts and skills related to a unit of study with they are currently learning. These concepts and skills are integrated into their script to tell a story.  Teachers who allow their students to demonstrate their mastery of concept and skills, as well as developing their communication skills through movie making, understand this information on a deeper level and do better on standardized tests.

The Apple I Movie is a great application for creating student documentaries and learning videos.  Video footage can be shot with an Apple mobile device such as an iPhone, iTouch, I Pad2, or through photo booth on an Apple desktop or laptop and imported into the iMovie application on an Apple laptop or desktop computer, and edited into the final version of a movie. Movies can be saved on a hard drive, thumb drive, burned on a DVD via iDVD , or posted on the web.  Movies made in this way are fast, easy, and fun!

# Animated Movies

Students can create animated movies by typing in text on Go Animate! http://goanimate.com and Xtranormal MovieMaker http://www.xtranormal.com. Students can create a free account on these websites and create short animated movies as projects that can be shared in class. Students can choose characters, a background and animation to appear in their narratives. Teachers find this web web application user-friendly, engaging, and a creative way to bring the curriculum alive.

# Podcasts

A podcast is a digital or electronic audio or video file that is released as episodes and can be downloaded (most commonly through web syndication) to a computer or mobile device such as a smartphone, I Touch or a tablet such as an I Pad. Podcasts can be used in the dissemination of audio or video broadcasts to the public. They can also be utilized to transform a written eBook into a audio-book by recording the book as it is read and saving it as an MP3 file.

Podcasts have several unique and practical uses in the realm of education. They can be created by educators or the students themselves for uniquely different purposes:

## A. Podcasts Created by Educators can be used for:

Weekly Previews to material that will be learned in class

A class lecture, lesson, or activity in audio or video formats

Student cross curricular, standard-based projects demonstrating mastery of key concepts and skills

Professional development and training videos (Webinars) to be posted on a website for teachers, staff, or students

Informational videos to be posted on a website

Audio-visual workshops to be presented at conferences

## B. Podcasts Created by Students as Projects:

A documentary about school or student life

Student advertisements about students running for Student Council positions

Videos about class field trips

A video project that demonstrates learning of key concepts in a unit of study such as a audio-visual presentation or documentary: some topics can include:

Videos presentations about historical events, places, people, debates

Videos about performing arts shows such as plays and musical performances

Videos about science labs, experiments, activities and projects (i.e. science fair project)

Audio-visual presentations about books, authors, short stories, and poems.

Audio recordings of music, songs, books, stories, and poems read out loud.

# Chapter 9

# You Tube

If any website has revolutionized the way we use movies and videos it is You Tube. You tube is a media streaming provider which "streams" video and audio, to its users. The term "streaming" refers to the manner in which media is delivered to the user. Media is constantly received and presented to users while being delivered to You Tube. The You Tube browser will display a movie or video before the entire file is delivered.

You Tube allows its users to stream in movies and videos that have be previously recorded or streamed in live over the Internet. The website uses a Flash based player to stream in live video. Common examples of live streaming occurs with live musical performances, news broadcasts, and important events such as the Olympics. Mobile devices such as tablets, smartphones, and I Pods can also stream in media files effortlessly.

You Tube has become an important media source for both educators and students in Education. Users have taken full advantage of You Tube by registering for a free account and setting up a "channel" where they can upload and host their media. Virtually anyone can create a channel for a multitude of purposes. Educators have used You Tube to allow other educators to access professional development workshops, seminars, and lectures about best practices and novel instructional strategies. Young and aspiring film-makers in high school and college have also used You Tube to host their movie, documentaries, and directorial projects. This website can also be utilized to:

-Students can use movies, videos, and animations to demonstrate their knowledge and comprehension of concepts and skills they have learned.

-Schools can post videos and movies to highlight and advertise their clubs, associations, sports team, musical and theatrical performances, and special events.

-Educators can post video lessons and resources to differentiate their curriculum and enhance their students' understanding of concepts and skills.

-Educators and students can set up a "channel" for school broadcasting such as television programs, news, documentaries, sports events, plays, concerts, lectures, discussions, and interviews.

# Chapter 10

# Comics

Comic strips and comic books are creative tools that can bring the curriculum to life. Both educators and students can utilize these tools for educational purposes. Educators can create animated lessons and activities to engage and motivate students to learn. Students can create animated movies, cartoons, comic strips and comic books to demonstrate mastery of content area concepts and skills. Students can develop stories, summaries, and demonstrate comprehension of standard-based concepts and skills through authentic projects using creative media.

Projects such as these help to differentiate the curriculum by giving students a variety of opportunities to communicate and express what they have learned in different ways. Comics are a creative outlet for students to demonstrate their mastery of concepts and skills they have learned and can be used in leu of an activity such as answering comprehension questions based on reading a text. Sometimes making a slight change or replacement in the learning task required by students can increase their engagement, work output and rate of completion tremendously!

**Comix  http://www.makebeliefscomix.com/Comix/** is a website students can use to generate simple comic strips. The online software allows students to create 2-dimensional comic strips by grabbing and dragging graphics, images, and dialogue bubbles to an already assembled comic strip template. Students can choose from a collection of characters, scenes, and objects. Students can email themselves or the educator the comic strips they work on and save a copy of the email to their computers or flash drives.  Students can collect them and produce a comic portfolio when they have amassed enough of them.

Educators can also use Comix as a resource for lessons.  This site contains over 250 blank comic and multi-purpose lesson templates that can be printed and used in any classroom for free!  Many lessons include writing prompts and ideas for stories students can use to practice their writing skills.  Educators can also create their own lessons and tailor them to specific standards-based content across the curriculum.

# TRANSFORMING
## the World of Education

The vision of the eClassroom 4 Teachers website is to help educators such as yourself, learn about the latest technology and how it can be integrated and applied as a powerful learning tool in the curriculum. eClassroom for Teachers was created and designed for educators to attain these technological skills. By integrating technology in the classroom, educators are able to teach their students how to use 21st century technological skills now and in the future.

## Visit Our Website at:

https://sites.google.com/site/eclassroom/
4teachers/Home

# Creating  Interactive Web Books

Many teachers I know are changing the face of education by using alternative methods to deliver a standards-based curriculum in a more interactive and engaging way by using technology as a tool in their instruction.   Websites can be transformed into easy to access storybooks or "Web Books"utilizing web pages as the pages of a storybook.  All the student needs is to create a website is a computer, internet access and a free web account such as Google Sites.

Websites are dynamic tools which allow teachers and students to write and publish not only what they know in terms of their understanding of knowledge and skills, but they also are given the opportunity to communicate and express their thoughts, ideas, and creativity in written form. Teachers and students are also able to integrate different technology tools into their websites such as videos, animation, audio recordings, music, or images to create their online web "books" and bring their stories to life.  Students, like teachers,  can also create websites on Google sites for free.

Printed in Great Britain
by Amazon